Brazen

*A Painting
&
Poetry Collection*

Edited by Keith Martin

Brazen, A Painting & Poetry Collection
Copyright © 2017 Griffith Moon. All rights reserved.
No part of this publication may be duplicated or
transmitted in any form without prior written consent from
the artist. Displaying such material without prior permission
is a violation of international copyright laws.

ISBN: 978-0-9993153-3-0
Library of Congress Control Number: 2017916231

Book Design by Sara Martinez
Cover Painting: "Ceiling of Gold", Oil, Gold on linen,
by Kimberly Brooks
Editorial by Keith Martin
Printed in the United States of America
First Printing, 2017

Brazen, an exhibition of new paintings by Kimberly Brooks
was held in the Fall of 2017 at the Zevitas Marcus Gallery
in Culver City

Published by Griffith Moon
Santa Monica, California
www.GriffithMoon.com

Brazen

*A Painting
&
Poetry Collection*

Brendan Constantine

Rich Ferguson

Marie Marandola

Luivette Resto

Paintings by Kimberly Brooks

Griffith Moon

Contents

Introduction by Keith Martin	...xv
Brendan Constantine	
Red Sugar Blue Smoke	...3
The Second Ovation Study	...9
KABOOM	...15
It's been Thursday for two weeks	...21
Rich Ferguson	
Just Moments After Eternity's Musicians Had Taken a Break to Retune Their Instruments	...29
She	...35
Side Effects	...41
When Wilhelm Röntgen Visits the Farm	...47
A World of Things	...53
Marie Marandola	
Talitha	...63
In Advance of the Sage Smudge	...69
If a Poet Writes About Herself in the Bathtub, and No One is Around to Care, Can She Still Call It a Poem?	...75
Luivette Resto	
Angel/Mother/Goddess	...83
The Myth of the Cave	...89
Contributor Biographies	...92

Introduction
by *Keith Martin*

*The wider the community of your heart,
the wider the community around you.*
—Henri Nouwen

When I read great poetry I am immersed completely, totally enthralled by the written word. As poet Paul Strand eloquently wrote, "Ink runs from the corners of my mouth. There is no happiness like mine. I have been eating poetry." Reading poetry is always personal, a connection with the author but also with the world at large. I feel that great poems should be shared and used as a narrative to counter the news we hear everyday. Nothing makes me happier than attending readings and hearing fresh, exciting poets. I attend readings all over LA on a search for new voices. Sharing their work makes me feel alive and plugged in to the heart beat of the city. I support and advocate for the LA literary community because I want to celebrate the diversity and enormous talent in my city.

I remember being overwhelmed in my teens spending two days in the Louvre in Paris. I felt that the museum had been curated to be a gift to Parisians. I returned home with a strong sense that supporting the arts was going to be my way of giving back to the city I live in too. I have been a patron of the arts since I began exploring the Santa Monica galleries in my 20's.

The Brazen live reading, along with the book you are now holding, began when I spotted Kimberly Brook's paintings online several years ago. I started posting her paintings on Facebook and Instagram paired with poems I had collected. Later, she contacted me and told me she was having an exhibit and asked me to assist her in creating a happening to coincide with her show. I invited a select group of badass L.A. poets to read at her closing party. I even went a step further: I had the poets create new works inspired by Kimberly's artwork, then paired each of those poems with one of Kimberly's paintings to best tell the story of her art. This book brings together her newest creations with brand new poems to create a masterpiece of connection.

Hopefully you are reading this book because you admire Kimberly's original paintings or have read the poets and want to see more. I respect their creative work very much and want their audience to dramatically expand. Because I think everyone should be reading great poetry and admiring fabulous art. The four poets in this book deserve massive success and admiration. I hope you love their poems as much as I loved editing this work and hosting the reading.

Keith Martin
Los Angeles, October 2017

Brendan Constantine

Blue Forest
44 x 36 in.
Oil on Linen

Red Sugar Blue Smoke

My power animal is prehistoric, so far
undiscovered. I wait for its bones
to be found. I'm not hopeful;
it was drawn to bright lights
and may have stood directly under the meteor,
blue head cocked like a microphone. I have
twenty-eight teeth and can't decide
if I'm a predator. I once killed a story
with tiny cuts, then buried it
under a tree. The guilt fed and sheltered me
for half a winter. My new landlady
is an astrologer/real-estate-agent who
refuses to say if my home can be trusted
with secrets. Her favorite nail polish is

a shade of dark red called 'Girl Against
The Whole Damn World.' I wonder
what color says, *I left my drink
next to an identical one and now I can't tell
which is mine?* Tomorrow is a blue vein
in the back of your hand. This isn't a figure
of speech but a fact of nature, like ink. Tomorrow is
also a powerful animal with undetermined markings.
Indeed it's probably camouflaged somewhere
near by. All we know for sure is it will be
eight letters long, the last resembling
a pair of fangs.

This poem first appeared in the journal 'Rattle,' 2016.

Portrait Hall
36 x 44 in.
Oil on Linen

The Second Ovation Study

was held in a small, unpainted room
with one chair and one table upon
which lay a toy flute. On entering,
most applicants quickly sat down,
took up the instrument and began
to play, though none appeared to
know any recognizable tune. Three
remained standing for the duration
of the study, as if awaiting instructions.
A few, maybe five, pocketed the flute
and one denied doing so, even after
being shown surveillance of the theft.
This, too, was the only applicant
to describe the exam as unpleasant.

Almost all reported a feeling of nostalgia,
a desire to connect with lost relations,
especially the dead. Apropos of this,
there were no deaths or injuries
during the study. This is remarkable
because several people did at some point
stand on the table with their eyes closed.
It has been determined they did so
unconsciously, in delight of the songs
they almost played.

Gods and Mountains
60 x 48 in.
Oil on Linen

KABOOM

I love the sound of molten lava
amplified to the level of punk
rock. It's my latest god. My last
was the shelf at Goodwill
marked USED MUSIC. Not
what it held, but the shelf itself,
the holy fact that every thrift shop
has one. I still fear its power,
but I don't do its work. My oldest
gods live on a mattress in the back
of my head; a man and woman —
junkies both — nodding out to
reruns of childhood. They rarely
interfere. Some nights the woman

will fumble the intercom, saying
*You should find that girl you liked
in preschool and ask if she's busy.*
Or the man will cry at the TV and
beg me to sing so he can cry harder.
Verily I tune them out. Brother,
I've heard the light and it's a Boom
Shaka Lacka. It's the earth boiling
into seven billion really expensive
microphones (I'm sure this time),
the roar of the crowd at Pompei.

Wall of Delight
44 x 36 in.
Oil on Linen

It's Been Thursday for two weeks now

and they've taken down all the paintings.
Thursday sucks. I suppose you like it,
I bet you think Thursday is innocent,
a bowl of flowers in milk. Well, we all
have our little Antarcticas. Personally,
the crack of ice hurts my eyes, makes me
want to crumple whatever I'm writing and
wait for a thaw, for a splash or trickle
(Not one seashell answers). When I lived
in space, I had a shorter name. Have you
been there? You'd know. Thursday isn't
a bowl of anything; it's the cup you find
under the bed, it's how long you marvel

at what's left, at the dark rule of sugar.
Remember when Thursday was just trying
to drink without spilling? My name changed
with every try, till I got it down. You're only
half as smart as you feel. Some Friday,
people will open their hands and find
cave paintings; great huntingscapes with
stick men and scribbly bears. Trust me,
I'm the one who always gets eaten. Speech
began as a way to tell people to chew
with their God damn mouths closed. That's
what Saturday and Sunday say, anyway.
But, they'll quote anything that distracts
from the wilderness of our first dreams –
white earth, wet flowers, two hairy people
who don't yet know what a day is.

Rich Ferguson

Hall of Eternity
30 x 24 in.
Oil on Linen

Just Moments After Eternity's Musicians Had Taken a Break to Retune Their Instruments

What I recall,
a long, silent hallway;
just moments after eternity's musicians
had taken a break
to retune their instruments.

What I recall,
a gracious home
leaning towards the lips
of tranquility—

a soon-to-be kiss
yearning to be
memorialized by elegance,
framed by hands
cut off from
the elbows of war.

Just outside
the front door—
pills of hate
swallowed by the bitter masses;
drugged and wailing shards
of amnesiac moonlight
preying upon hopeless lovers;
reason sleepwalking
into the wide-open mouths
of guns.

Those left alive and unscathed
tattoo their memories
with shadows, nightmares, rubble.

A way to remember
what they no longer wish to remember.

Crown of Thorns
24 x 18 in.
Oil on Linen

She

She is an amnesiac moon,
a lunatic laundromat
robbing me of my quarters.
She has
tombstones tarot cards;
ties my pulse
into a hangman's knot.
She is a forever leaving ship;
my arms ache
from perpetually waving goodbye.
She is a nightmare
strapped to a boomerang;
the rush of blood before the injury,
the jagged scar preceding the wound.

She tells me
the knife
she's plunged into my back
will only be there temporarily,
as long as it takes
to find someone else
to carry it for her.
In the center of my chest,
she builds a church
of the disassembled—
a mangled and bloody gospel
bombed on unholy water,
tearing me apart
one heartbeat at a time.
She tells me
this is how she loves me.
She tells me
whatever I do
with my very next breath,
don't say no.

Castle Tapestry
44 x 36 in.
Oil, Gold Leaf on Linen

Side Effects

Side effects may include bone fractures, hair loss.
Unmappable and unconquerable sadness.
Dizziness of dynamism. Diminished well-being.
Optimism may experience difficulties in achieving orgasm.

Visual, aural, and tactile hallucinations have been
known to occur. Heart may become hacked, held
for ransom. Your shadow may assume the shape of a
smoking gun.

Additional side effects may include acne, crying spells.
Bone marrow transformed into dead sparrows.

Any and all butterflies in your stomach may flap wings, create inner hurricanes, tornadoes. Un tic-toc timelines of once stable quantum systems, alternative facts generated throughout the brain.

Allergic reactions have been known to happen when mixing casual conversation with politics.

You may become thin-skinned, susceptible to rage. Especially with matters concerning race, gender, climate change, and FBI investigations.

Suppression of the body's ability to generate open-mindedness may lead to overeating and Fox News binge watching.

Innovation, fresh ideas, new approaches to life have been known to experience flatulence.

Infrequent side effects may include mouth and anus reversed, so all you do is talk shit, and shit talk.

When mixed with blackmail and highly dubious foreign dignitaries, benevolence has been known to become an embezzler, money launderer, backstabber.

Skin clammy with selfishness, pustules on politeness, infected equanimity. Please see your doctor if you experience cruelty for more than 72 hours.

Fatal side effects may include supporting terrorist organizations such as Neo-Nazis and the KKK. Other serious events may include anaphylactic shock of compassion and sheer intelligence.

When properly used, social media activism is usually well tolerated, but if it leads to uncontrollable Twitter bullying, internal bleeding has been known to occur.

Drowsiness, dry mouth. Increased susceptibility to fake-news infection.

Prolonged usage may lead to diminished sight in your third eye. Inner doors of perception may change their locks; leave you shut out of your own consciousness.

Muscle spasms, rashes, backaches. The once honeyed milk of human kindness may leave a fishy taste on your tongue.

Seizures, strokes, problems with memory attention. Which may cause you to forget all of this come morning.

Prince
20 x 16 in.
Oil on Linen

When Wilhelm Röntgen Visits the Farm

When Wilhelm Röntgen visits the farm
the moon jumps over the cow;
sheep play ping-pong
with unstable isotopes;
geese and goats get stoned,
create cathode-ray light shows.

When Wilhelm Röntgen visits the farm
pigs wallow in radioactive baths;
ducks contemplate the phenomena
of spreading oil drops on water;
backhoes harvest the souls of all beings.

The farmer awakens
to a fluorescent light
beside him in bed;
he witnesses
the X-ray'ed bones
of his wife—

shimmering brighter than tractor headlights.

When Wilhelm Röntgen visits the farm
rainbows crossdress as gamma rays;
horses gallop through electrostatic fields;
corn crops spike silky hair,
pierce ears,
crank punk rock.

And as
the farmer and his wife—
upon their creaky bed,
in a drab pre-dawn room—
plow the aged furrows
of one another's bodies,
weariness melts away;
visible hearts beat faster, brighter—
everything glows.

Chess Game
9 x 12 in.
Oil, Gold Leaf on Linen

A World of Things

Things we've said under our breath.

Things people have said with their last dying breath.

Things that drive people to drink.

Things that made Jesus think, "Maybe I'm in the wrong line of business..."

Things you can only find in Detroit.

Things that make you jump for joy.

Things that make people jump from the Golden Gate Bridge.

Things you get stuck between your teeth.

Things you've stuck in your ear, up your nose, or up your butt.

Things that change from ugly to beautiful.

Things that frighten you, things that enliven you.

Things to help raise your credit score, things to help lower your cholesterol.

Things organisms have done to adapt.

Things that make certain men become priests.

Things that make certain women wrestle alligators.

Things serial killers think about.

Things you find in a dead man's pockets, things you find in your own pockets.

Things named after Greek Gods, things people have done in the name of God.

Things that cause acne, things that cause cancer.

Things to consider before having a baby.

Things to consider before joining the French Foreign Legion.

Things you'd do if you had wings.

Things you'd do if you had the Green Lantern's power ring.

Things to help clear out your aura, things to help clear out of your orifices.

Things you should always buy generic.

Things you've always wanted to know, but were afraid to ask.

Things people have done under the influence of love.

Things people have done under the influence of drugs.

Things you see when staring up at the clouds.

Things your pets do when you're not around.

Things you can smoke, things you can recycle.

Things to make your car run better.

Things you find on the side of the road, things you find washed up on the beach.

Things you build. Things you compete for.

Things you do when you're alone in your room.

Things you can burn, things you can save.

Things to say to get a girl wet, things to say to get a guy hard.

Things to say to get kicked off jury duty.

Things you can carry, things you can hide.

Things that decay, things that rejuvenate.

Things you put into compost piles, things that live under your skin.

Things you find around Jim Morrison's grave.

Things your doctor won't tell you, things your parents won't tell you.

Things your lover won't tell you, things your best friend won't tell you.

Things the major corporations won't tell you, things the government won't tell you.

Will *never* tell you.

Marie Marandola

Talitha
20 x 16 in.
Oil on Linen

Talitha

I live for the winter.
For the chance to build myself
with thick sweaters
and shapeless coats, while the world sheds
her pretense of trees.

Show me your barren face, World.
Help me obscure mine
behind your whip
of stinging wind.
Leave me chapped
and blurry and bulky
with wool. I am weary

of my smallness, of the food
that I don't want to eat
as I stand outside Wells Fargo
on a February Sunday.
Wearing only one glove, bare fingers
numbing against my cigarette's filter,
I'm trying to grow full
of smoke and freezing air,
trying to become
large that way.

I want a voice
that will echo deep against the empty
hillsides. I want to wave my hand
in front of the public restroom faucet,
have it recognize my presence
and respond. I want to walk
past darkened driveways and be bathed
in sudden light.

I only want to open doors.

Blue Angels
24 x 18 in.
Oil, Silver Leaf on Linen

In Advance of the Sage Smudge

After René Magritte's The Seducer *which he described as a "pictorial solution" to the "problem of water."*

The problem of water
is that we are made of it

and what we are made of
is never enough.

We used to sit on the edge
of the hot tub, fully dressed

but for our bare feet, our pants
hiked to our knees. We read,

talked, kissed, tested the heat
this way. You told me you meant

the things you said, but only
at the time that you said them.

Last night, the shimmer of you
sailed into my sleeping,

real enough to taste. So this
is what it's come to: drought

and haunting. In the dream
I was wearing flannel. In the dream

you told me not to say *I want*
anymore. The wet sidewalk

smelled of incense. Wispy cacti
twisted like vines

up the fronts of the houses.
In the dream the clouds

rolled in, and with them
giant flying termites. I batted

their red exo-skulls
away with my hands.

I picked up the free bookshelf
someone had left by the curb,

and carried it until it incinerated,
until my eyelashes all fell out

and landed in my mouth
and turned to glitter. In the dream,

I was slicing watermelon
into perfect circles.

I passed one to you, and you
smashed your face through it, wore

the jagged rind
like a juicy halo.

I want, I said.

Gilded Cage
36 x 44 in.
Oil, Gold Leaf on Linen

If a Poet Writes About Herself in the Bathtub, and No One is Around to Care, Can She Still Call It a Poem?

I'm sitting in the big Jacuzzi tub
in my parents' bathroom,
slick bare skin on slick porcelain.
Spearmint-and-eucalyptus-scented bubbles
dance around my thighs.
I am even drinking wine.

The tub has been gathering dust
since I moved out of the house years ago.
Like a baby grand piano
sitting in a foyer.

Like the poetry we teach in school.
It's gone past the prime of a teenage girl
hearing her body's secrets whispered
by a handheld showerhead.

But tonight I'm here
nursing the sting of a professor
who told me poetry
shouldn't be autobiographical—
as though turning experience into art
is masturbatory, a transgression:
something that can't give pleasure
to anyone but me.

Well.

Then consider this poem a match I struck
just for the smell of sulfur.

Consider this poem a pirate
hoarding oranges while the gold sits idly by.

Consider this poem a bank robbery
in the wake of an orgasm.

Luivette Resto

Angel/Mother/Goddess
60 x 48 in.
Oil on Linen

Angel/Mother/Goddess

I have been called all three
because I had to be:
>the holy trinity of femininity

Angel by the nuns and priests
when I behaved properly during communion
carrying tasteless wafers to the altar

Little angel by visiting relatives from the island
reciting a script of English responses
to prove how well we are doing in the mainland

>Mother, ma, mommy, momma,
>mamá, mama baby, moma,
>gimme, s/he started it, I didn't do it

Mother, her name when I seek comfort in her hugs
when I fantasize who I need her to be
instead of the woman she is

> Oh, thank the goddess
> Goddess bless you
> One nation under a goddess

Goddess from the mouths of men
after I leave their beds
> mutual bodies rightfully tired.

The Myth of the Cave
44 x 60 in.
Oil on Linen

The Myth of the Cave

Imaginary men and women
became legendary
when they spoke about it
if Don Lozada was talking
it was where our ancestors survived winters so cold
icicles were used as weapons to fight off
ferocious animals twice their size
if Abuelita Santiago had the floor
it was the genesis of our family's legacy
en las montañas de San Lorenzo
when our great-great- great-great grand uncle
became the cave's first governor
if Tío Songo didn't take a smoke break after dinner

it was where neighbors ceased to be enemies
leaving rhythms from their feet and bodies as offerings
around a fire made from the same palms
pounding the drums.

Contributor Biographies

Brendan Constantine's work has appeared in *Prairie Schooner, FIELD, Ploughshares, Virginia Quarterly,* and *Ninth Letter,* among other journals. His most recent collection is *Dementia, My Darling* (2016 Red Hen Press). He has received grants and commissions from the Getty Museum, James Irvine Foundation, and the National Endowment for the Arts. He currently teaches poetry at the Windward School and regularly offers classes to hospitals, foster homes, veterans, and the elderly.

Pushcart-nominated poet, Rich Ferguson has shared the stage with Patti Smith, Wanda Coleman, Moby, and other esteemed artists. He is a featured performer in the film *What About Me?* His poetry has been widely published, and his spoken word videos have appeared in international film festivals. His poetry collection *8th & Agony* is out on Punk Hostage Press. His debut novel, *New Jersey Me,* is available through Rare Bird Books.

Marie Marandola is a badass feminist poet who received her MFA from Sarah Lawrence College. She is an editor for the literary press *Meow Meow Pow Pow*, and the former poetry editor of *Lumina Journal*. Her work has appeared in *Poetry International*, *Fairy Tale Review*, *Lunch Ticket*, and *Dressing Room Poetry Journal*, amongst others, and her poem "Poet Groupie" won the Academy of American Poets University Prize for Sarah Lawrence College in 2016. She now lives in San Diego, where she remains in the habit of picking up fallen bits of trees and giving them to people.

Luivette Resto, a mother, teacher, poet, and Wonder Woman fanatic, was born in Aguas Buenas, Puerto Rico but proudly raised in the Bronx. Her two books of poetry *Unfinished Portrait* and *Ascension* have been published by Tia Chucha Press. She is a CantoMundo fellow and has served as a contributing poetry editor for *Kweli Journal*. Some of her latest work can be read in *Entropy Magazine*, *Coiled Serpent anthology*, *Altadena Anthology 2015 & 2016*, and an anthology of Afro-Latino poetry titled *¡Manteca!* published by Arte Público Press. Currently, she lives in the Los Angeles area with her three children.

Keith Martin is a community organizer and long time supporter of the LA literary community. He served on the Los Angeles poet laureate selection committee. He was appointed by Los Angeles Mayor Eric Garcetti to the LA County Metropolitan Transit Authority Citizens Advisory Council. He serves on the Clinica Romero executive executive board as fundraising chair and homeless patient advocate. He is the Chairperson of the Golden State Bonsai Federation committee at the Huntington Library and Gardens Bonsai Pavillion. He volunteers as a Crossing Angel for CicLAvia and also at Beyond Baroque literary center in Venice.

Los Angeles-based artist, Kimberly Brooks, integrates figuration and abstraction to explore a variety of subjects dealing with history, memory and identity. Brooks has solo exhibitions throughout the United States and her work has been showcased in juried exhibitions including curators from the Whitney Museum of American Art, The Museum of Modern Art, Los Angeles County Museum of Art. The paintings featured in this book were first shown at the Zevitas Marcus Gallery in Culver City Fall 2017. www.kimberlybrooks.com

CPSIA information can be obtained at www.ICGtesting.com
Printed in the USA
BVIW12n0812270718
522569BV00005BA/9